P9-CRN-936

The Christian and Witnessing

Bringing Words of Hope to the World Around You

STEP 7

Bill Bright

NewLife
PUBLICATIONS
A MINISTRY OF CAMPUS CRUSADE FOR CHRIST

Ten Basic Steps Toward Christian Maturity
Step 7: The Christian and Witnessing

Published by
New*Life* Publications
100 Lake Hart Drive
Orlando, FL 32832-0100

© 1994, Bill Bright. All rights reserved. No part of this publication may be reproduced, stored in a retrieval system, or transmitted in any form or by any means, except in the case of brief quotations printed in articles or reviews, without prior permission in writing from the publisher.

Printed in the United States of America.

Four Spiritual Laws © 1965, Campus Crusade for Christ International. All rights reserved. The *Four Spiritual Laws* cannot be copied in any form without permission from NewLife Publications.

ISBN: 1-56399-036-9

Thomas Nelson Inc., Nashville, Tennessee, is the exclusive distributor of this book to the trade markets in the United States and the District of Columbia.

Distributed in Canada by Campus Crusade for Christ of Canada, Surrey, B.C.

Unless otherwise indicated, all Scripture references are from the *New International Version*, © 1973, 1978, 1984 by the International Bible Society. Published by Zondervan Bible Publishers, Grand Rapids, Michigan.

Scripture quotations designated TLB are from *The Living Bible*, © 1971 by Tyndale House Publishers, Wheaton, Illinois.

Scripture portions used in the *Four Spiritual Laws* are from the *New American Standard Bible*, © 1960, 1962, 1963, 1968, 1971, 1972, 1975, 1977 by the Lockman Foundation, La Habra, California.

> Any royalties from this book or the many other books by Bill Bright are dedicated to the glory of God and designated to the various ministries of Campus Crusade for Christ/*NewLife2000*.

For more information, write:

L.I.F.E.—P. O. Box 40, Flemmington Markets, 2129, Australia
Campus Crusade for Christ of Canada—Box 300, Vancouver, B.C., V6C 2X3, Canada
Campus Crusade for Christ—Fairgate House, King's Road, Tyseley, Birmingham, B11 2AA, England
Lay Institute for Evangelism—P. O. Box 8786, Auckland 3, New Zealand
Campus Crusade for Christ—Alexandra, P. O. Box 0205, Singapore 9115, Singapore
Great Commission Movement of Nigeria—P. O. Box 500, Jos, Plateau State Nigeria, West Africa
Campus Crusade for Christ International—100 Sunport Lane, Orlando, FL 32809, USA

Contents

Acknowledgments

The *Ten Basic Steps Toward Christian Maturity* series was a product of necessity. As the ministry of Campus Crusade for Christ expanded rapidly to scores of campuses across America, thousands of students committed their lives to Christ—several hundred on a single campus. Individual follow-up of all new converts soon became impossible. Who was to help them grow in their new-found faith?

A Bible study series designed for new Christians was desperately needed—a study that would stimulate individuals and groups to explore the depths and the riches of God's Word. Although several excellent studies were available, we felt the particular need of new material for these college students.

In 1955, I asked several of my fellow staff associates to assist me in the preparation of Bible studies that would stimulate both evangelism and Christian growth in a new believer. The contribution by campus staff members was especially significant because of their constant contact with students in introducing them to Christ and meeting regularly with them to disciple them. Thus, the *Ten Basic Steps Toward Christian Maturity* was the fruit of our combined labor.

Since that modest beginning, many other members of the staff have contributed generously. On occasion, for example, I found myself involved in research and writing sessions with several of our staff, all seminary graduates, some with advanced degrees and one with his doctorate in theology. More important, all were actively engaged in "winning, building, and sending men" for Christ.

For this latest edition, I want to thank Don Tanner for his professional assistance in revising, expanding, and editing the contents. I also want to thank Joette Whims and Jean Bryant for their extensive help and for joining Don and me in the editorial process.

A Personal Word

"Y ou must bring a lot of happiness into this world," exclaimed the young businessman with tears of joy and gratitude in his eyes. I had just finished sharing the *Four Spiritual Laws* booklet with him, and he had prayed with me receiving Christ as his Savior and Lord.

"My wife and I have been looking for God for several years," he said. "I'm going to take this booklet with me so I can help her receive Christ, too."

The words of this joyful young Christian have come to my mind again and again: "You must bring a lot of happiness into this world."

Since I received Christ as my Savior and Lord in 1944, I have had the exciting privilege of "bringing a lot of happiness into this world" by sharing the Lord Jesus Christ with many millions of students and lay people around the world. On the basis of their remarkable response, I am deeply convinced that the world is more ready for the gospel of Christ today than ever before.

With a world so ready, we cannot afford to sit back and hope they will be reached. Our relatively few full-time ministers of the gospel, no matter how gifted and dedicated they may be, will not be able to accomplish the task alone. We too, as lay men and women and boys and girls, have the privilege—and

responsibility—of participating with our living Lord in the fulfill-
ment of His Great Commission in our generation.

Jesus promised, "Follow me and I will make you fishers of men."
It is our responsibility to follow Him and obey Him. He will do the
rest. It is His responsibility to make us fishers of men.

My prayer is that this study will bless and enrich your life and
increase your effectiveness as a personal witness for our Lord. I
assure you that there is no experience in life more exciting and
spiritually rewarding than helping to bring a lot of happiness into
this world by introducing people to Christ.

What This Study Will Do for You

Have you talked with someone about Jesus Christ today? During the past week? Or month? Or year? How many have you spoken with regarding their salvation since you became a Christian?

If I could show you how you can share your faith often, successfully, and with confidence without alienating others or becoming someone you really don't want to be, would you be interested?

Witnessing for our Lord is something we all know we should do, yet we frequently shrink from it. We feel we would be intruding into someone else's life, and it seems not only threatening but also blatantly presumptuous. We fear offending the other person; we fear being rejected; we fear doing an inadequate job of representing our Lord. And we fear being branded a fanatic.

So we remain silent, and we pray that God will use someone else to get His message to those around us who do not know Him.

If you have struggled with these fears, I have good news for you! Christians like you, from all walks of life, are learning how to share their faith in Christ without fear.

For almost fifty years I have been involved in training Christians across the country and around the world to share their

❖

This practical study will help you learn to share your faith with confidence.

faith in Christ in a way that can produce more fruit. While I am encouraged at the large numbers of Christians who are beginning to witness with confidence, our studies show that as many as 98 percent of believers still are not witnessing effectively for our Savior.

Sharing With Confidence

If you are one of these, this practical study, prepared especially for you, will help you learn to share your faith with confidence in the power of the Holy Spirit.

You will benefit from this study in two ways:

First, *by learning how to witness more effectively.*

Many devout Christians fail miserably in their efforts to introduce others to Christ simply because they do not know how to go about it. In this study you will see Christ's example as a witness and discover what made Him effective. You also will learn vital steps to personal preparation for successful witnessing.

Second, *by discovering the secret to God's power in sharing your faith.*

Hebrews 4:12 says:

> The Word of God is living and active. Sharper than any double-edged sword, it penetrates even to dividing soul and spirit . . . it judges the thoughts and attitudes of the heart.

The early disciples learned to rely on the resources of God's Word, prayer, and the Holy Spirit as they spread the Good News of Christ. In this study you will learn how to use the power of God's Word in sharing your faith. You will discover how to make prayer a vital part of your witnessing, and you will learn how to understand and trust in the Holy Spirit's leading as you tell others about the Savior.

Is fear keeping you from sharing your faith? The principles you are about to consider have been learned on the front line of experience and have changed multitudes of silent, guilt-ridden Christians into radiant witnesses for our Lord. I assure you that if you apply the proven concepts presented in this study, you too will develop the confidence to become more effective in witnessing to those in your circle of influence.

Foundation for Faith

Step 7: The Christian and Witnessing is part of the *Ten Basic Steps Toward Christian Maturity,* a time-tested study series designed to provide you with a sure foundation for your faith. Hundreds of thousands have benefited from this Bible study series during the almost forty years since it was first published in its original form.

When you complete Step 7, I encourage you to continue your study with the rest of the Steps.

If you are a new Christian, the *Ten Basic Steps* will acquaint you with the major doctrines of the Christian faith. By applying the principles you will learn, you will grow spiritually and find solutions to problems you are likely to face as a new believer.

If you are a mature Christian, you will discover the tools you need to help others receive Christ and grow in their faith. Your own commitment to our Lord will be affirmed, and you will discover how to develop an effective devotional and study plan.

This series includes an individual booklet for the introductory study and one for each of the ten Steps. These study guides correlate with the expanded and updated *Handbook for Christian Maturity* and *Ten Basic Steps Leader's Guide.*

Each Step reveals a different facet of the Christian life and truth, and each contains lessons for study that can be used during your personal quiet time or in a group setting.

I encourage you to pursue the study of Step 7 with an open, eager mind. As you read, continually pray that God will show you how to relate the principles you learn to your own situation. Begin to apply them on a daily basis, and you will experience the exciting adventure of witnessing for Christ in the power of the Holy Spirit.

How to Use This Study

On page 13 of this Step, you will find the preparatory article, "Take the Challenge; Experience the Adventure." The article will give you a clear perspective on the exciting adventure of witnessing for Christ. Read it carefully before you begin Lesson 1. Review it prayerfully during your study.

This Step contains six lessons plus a "Recap" or review. The study concludes with important information on how to share Christ with others and a reproduction of the *Four Spiritual Laws*. Be sure to read this material and make its principles your own.

Each lesson is divided into two sections: the Bible Study and the Life Application. Begin by noting the Objective for the lesson you are studying. The Objective states the main goal for your study. Keep it in mind as you continue through the lesson.

Take time to memorize the referenced Scripture verses. Learn each one by writing it on a small card to carry with you. You can buy cards for these verses at any bookstore or print shop, or you can make your own by using filing cards. Review daily the verses you have memorized.

Our Lord has commanded that we learn His Word. Proverbs 7:1–3 reminds us:

> My son, keep my words and
> store up my commands within

Your most important objective is not to acquire knowledge, but to meet with God in a loving, personal way.

you. Keep my commands and you will live; guard my teachings as the apple of your eye. Bind them on your fingers; write them on the tablet of your heart.

As you use the verses you have memorized and claim God's promises, you will experience the joy, victory, and power that God's Word gives to your Christian walk. When you have finished all the studies in the entire series, you will be able to develop your own Bible study, continuing to use a systematic method for memorizing God's Word.

How to Study the Lessons

Casual Bible reading uncovers valuable spiritual facts that lie near the surface. But understanding the deeper truths requires study. Often the difference between reading and studying is a pen and notepad.

Every lesson in this study covers an important topic and gives you an opportunity to record your answers to the questions. Plan to spend a minimum of thirty minutes each day—preferably in the morning—in Bible study, meditation, and prayer.

Remember, the most important objective and benefit of a quiet time or Bible study is not to acquire knowledge or accumulate biblical information but to meet with God in a loving, personal way.

Here are some suggestions to help you in your study time:

◆ Plan a specific time and place to work on these studies. Make an appointment with God; then keep it.

◆ Use a pen or pencil, your Bible, and this booklet.

◆ Begin with prayer for God's presence, blessing, and wisdom.

◆ Meditate on the Objective to determine how it fits into your circumstances.

◆ Memorize the suggested verses.

◆ Proceed to the Bible study, trusting God to use it to teach you. Prayerfully anticipate His presence with you. Work carefully, reading the Scripture passages and thinking through the questions. Answer each as completely as possible.

◆ When you come to the Life Application, answer the questions honestly and begin to apply them to your own life.

◆ Prayerfully read through the lesson again and reevaluate your Life Application answers. Do they need changing? Or adjusting?

◆ Review the memory verses.

◆ Consider the Objective again and determine if it has been accomplished. If not, what do you need to do?

◆ Close with a prayer of thanksgiving, and ask God to help you grow spiritually in the areas He has specifically revealed to you.

◆ When you complete the first six lessons of this Step, spend some extra time on the Recap to make sure you understand every lesson thoroughly.

◆ If you need more study of this Step, ask God for wisdom again and go through whatever lesson(s) you need to review, repeating the process until you do understand and are able to apply the truths to your own life.

These studies are not intended as a complete development of Christian beliefs. However, a careful study of the material will give you, with God's help, a sufficient understanding of how you can know and apply God's plan for your life. The spiritual truths contained here will help you meet with our Lord Jesus Christ in an intimate way and discover the full and abundant life that Jesus promised (John 10:10).

Do not rush through the lessons. Take plenty of time to think through the questions. Meditate on them. Absorb the truths presented, and make the application a part of your life. Give God a chance to speak to you, and let the Holy Spirit teach you. As you spend time with our Lord in prayer and study, and as you trust and obey Him, you will experience the amazing joy of His presence (John 14:21).

Take the Challenge; Experience the Adventure

Frequently in my travels around the world, I visit with our staff and meet with thousands of pastors and laymen. On one occasion while meeting with a group of Christian leaders, I shared some of the highlights of the great worldwide spiritual harvest taking place today.

One of the leaders interrupted me. "I'm thrilled with your report," he said, "but to be very frank with you, I have not seen that kind of activity myself. Why am I not having a more fruitful ministry?"

Perhaps you are asking yourself the same question. Through this study, I want to help you be fruitful in your witness for our Lord wherever you are, wherever you go, and under all circumstances.

Today we live in a world of rapid and radical change. Men's hearts are filled with fear and dread, frustration and despair. Mankind has proven incapable of coping with the pressing problems of our time: the population explosion, the pollution of the environment, the rising tide of crime and violence, sexual rebellion, alcoholism, drug addiction, abortion, pornography, urban sprawl, and widespread political, social, and moral decay.

What an hour for Christians to become involved in the greatest spiritual harvest since New Testament times! This dark hour

The most exciting and spiritually rewarding experience in life is the adventure of fishing for people.

in the affairs of mankind is an hour of destiny, a time of unprece-
dented opportunity for Christians. This is the hour for which we
were born—to set in motion a mighty, sweeping spiritual revolution
that will turn the tide and reveal to mankind that the glorious gospel
of our Lord Jesus Christ offers the basic solutions to every problem
facing mankind.

If I had the privilege of writing a news story about the greatest
events of all the centuries, one of the most important would be a
meeting on a mountain near Galilee where a small group of men
were commanded to carry God's love and forgiveness to a lost and
dying world.

The Greatest Challenge

On this mountain these men received the greatest challenge ever
given to mankind, by the greatest Person who ever lived, concern-
ing the greatest power ever revealed and the greatest promise ever
recorded. I refer, of course, to the Great Commission of our Lord
Jesus Christ, which He gave to His disciples and through them to
us. He said:

> I have been given all authority in heaven and earth.
> Therefore go and make disciples in all the nations, bap-
> tizing them into the name of the Father and of the Son
> and of the Holy Spirit, and then teach these new disciples
> to obey all the commands I have given you; and be sure
> of this—that I am with you always, even to the end of the
> world (Matthew 28:18–20, TLB).

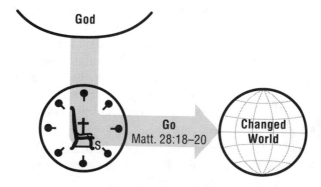

Later, on the Mount of Olives, our Lord gave His final word to His disciples and to us before He ascended to the Father. He said:

> When the Holy Spirit has come upon you, you will receive power to testify about me with great effect, to the people in Jerusalem, throughout Judea, in Samaria, and to the ends of the earth, about my death and resurrection (Acts 1:8, TLB).

Had these meetings not been held and had our Lord's command and promise not been given, you would not now be experiencing the love, forgiveness, joy, and purpose of God's matchless grace available to all who believe in Christ. In fact, I would not be writing this message.

The Focus of Jesus' Ministry

The Great Commission was the focus of Jesus' ministry on this earth. The fifth chapter of Luke records an incident in the life of a seasoned fisherman—Simon Peter. He and his fellow workers had spent the entire night casting and gathering their nets but had not caught a single fish.

Jesus observed these men as they were washing their nets and asked Peter to push out a little into the water so He could sit in the boat and speak to the crowds that were pressing around Him.

When He had finished speaking, Jesus made a promise to this fisherman—a promise that I believe Peter, weary from his futile night of fishing, initially thought foolish. Jesus told Peter to go out a little further and let down his nets. If he did so, he would catch fish. Luke records Peter's response and what happened as a result.

> "Sir," Simon [Peter] replied, "we worked hard all night and didn't catch a thing. But if you say so, we'll try again." And this time their nets were so full that they began to tear! A shout for help brought their partners in the other boat and soon both boats were filled with fish and on the verge of sinking (Luke 5:5–7, TLB).

Jesus told the fishermen who were so awestruck with this demonstration of His power, "From now on you'll be fishing for the souls of men!"

They were so overwhelmed with the presence and power of Jesus that they left their occupation to follow Him.

The most exciting and spiritually rewarding experience in life is the adventure of fishing for people. As you follow the Lord's instruction, your net too can be filled—even if you have never yet introduced anyone to Christ—even if you may be skeptical like Peter. But if you are also obedient like Peter, the Lord Jesus will honor you with the response of many people to your witness.

Why We Witness

"I think a man's religion is so personal we shouldn't discuss it."

"I don't like people who are dogmatic and fanatical about religion. They try to force their views on everybody they meet."

"Well, I have my own religion, and I'm happy with it."

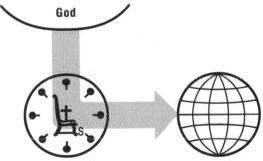

Objective: To understand the reasons to witness for Christ

Read: Galatians 1 and 2

Memorize: 2 Corinthians 5:14,15

Perhaps you have heard comments like these from someone you know. Or even made them yourself before you became a believer.

During approximately fifty years of sharing Christ and training others to do the same, I have found no biblical rationale to justify fearing those responses as a reason for not witnessing.

In fact, the need for people to hear the Good News of God's love and forgiveness is a matter of life and death. The writer of Ecclesiastes observes:

> Death is the destiny of every man; the living should take this to heart (Ecclesiastes 7:2).

Man's self-will is characterized by an attitude of active rebellion or passive indifference. Because of sin, he is by nature degenerate and corrupt, destitute of God's love, undeserving of His forgiveness, and so destined to death—eternal separation from God. But Christ does not want anyone to perish, but wants everyone to come to repentance (2 Peter 3:9).

He placed such high value on the human soul that He personally gladly exchanged the perfection of heaven for a life of poverty, suffering, shame, and death to seek and to save what was lost (Luke 19:10).

From His earliest youth and throughout His life, Jesus clearly understood His mission and purpose. His concern for the lost was so deep that at times the flood of compassionate tears rolled down His face. Jesus, the manliest of men, wept. Similarly, Paul pleaded night and day with everyone who would listen to be reconciled to God.

Since then, people of every century and many walks of life have had a heart of compassion for those who are living apart from God. Great spiritual leaders such as John Wesley, D. L. Moody, and Billy Sunday dedicated their lives to reaching people with the message of hope.

When one young missionary who had been sent home because of illness was asked why he was so eager to get back to his people, he said, "Because I cannot sleep for thinking about them."

Our Lord has commissioned each of us to share the Good News and "seek the lost." He said, "Go and make disciples of all nations"; and, "Go into all the world and preach the good news to all creation" (Matthew 28:19; Mark 16:15). It is our greatest calling, then, to share the love and forgiveness He has given us with those who have never received Him as their Savior and Lord.

From my personal experiences and studies of God's Word, five key concepts have been made clear to me—concepts that impact the lives of every Christian.

Christ has given a clear command to every Christian.

Jesus Christ's last command to the Christian community was to make disciples. This command, which the church calls the Great Commission, was not intended merely for the eleven remaining disciples, or just for the apostles, or for those in present times who may have the gift of evangelism. This command is the responsibility of every man and woman who professes faith in Christ as Lord.

Men and women are lost without Jesus Christ.

Jesus said, "I am the way and the truth and the life. No one comes to the Father, except through me" (John 14:6). God's Word also reminds us, "There is salvation in no one else! Under all heaven there is no other name for men to call upon to save them" (Acts 4:12, TLB).

Men and women are truly lost without Jesus Christ. He is the only way to bridge the gap between man and God. Without Him, people cannot know God and have no hope of eternal life.

Rather than being "not interested," the people of the world are truly hungry for the gospel.

One of the greatest misconceptions held by Christians today is that men and women do not want to know God. But wherever I go around the world, I find ample proof that just the opposite is true. The Holy Spirit has created a hunger for God in the hearts of millions.

I have discovered that at least 25 to 50 percent of nonbelievers are ready to receive Christ in most parts of the world if properly approached, one on one, by a trained Spirit-empowered witness. And I believe that among that number may be some of your own family members, a neighbor or a co-worker, or a person you do not yet know to whom God may lead you. They are ready to hear a clear and simple presentation of the Good News of God's love and forgiveness.

Jesus said, "The fields are ripe unto harvest." Can we afford to be selfish with the gospel when such overwhelming evidence shows that so many people are hungry for God? By sharing our faith in Christ with others, we can help change our world for our Lord.

We Christians have in our possession the greatest gift available to mankind: God's gift of eternal life, which we received with Jesus Christ at our spiritual birth (John 3:16).

Christ is risen! We serve a living Savior! He not only lives within us in all His resurrection power, but He also has assured us of eternal life. He died on the cross in our place for our sin, then rose from the dead. We have direct fellowship with God through Jesus Christ. And this fellowship, this peace, this gift of eternal life, is available to all who receive Him.

The love of Jesus Christ for us, and our love for Him, compels us to share Him with others.

Jesus said, "The one who obeys me is the one who loves me..." (John 14:21, TLB). In other words, He measures our love for Him by the extent and genuineness of our obedience to Him. As we obey, He promises He will reveal Himself to us.

> Because he loves me, My Father will love him; and I
> will too, and I will reveal myself to him (John 14:21, TLB).

What are we to obey? When it comes to witnessing, we have the specific commandment from Jesus Christ to go into all the world with the Good News.

Helping to fulfill the Great Commission is both a duty and a privilege. We witness because we love Christ. We witness because He loves us. We witness because we want to honor and obey Him. We witness because He gives us a special love for others.

God wants you to witness because of the benefits He offers to those who receive Christ:

◆ They become children of God.

◆ Their bodies become temples of God.

◆ All of their sins are forgiven.

◆ They begin to experience the peace and love of God.

◆ They receive God's direction and purpose for their lives.

◆ They experience the power of God to change their lives.

◆ They have assurance of eternal life.

God also wants you to witness because of the benefits you will receive. Witnessing will stimulate your spiritual growth, lead you to pray and study God's Word, and encourage you to depend on Christ. You will experience the tremendous privilege and honor of representing Jesus to the world (2 Corinthians 5:20).

The Holy Spirit came to provide the power for you to do so (Acts 1:8). Wouldn't you like to share with someone else the most valuable thing you have?

All over the world, I have asked two questions of Christians, young and old, rich and poor, new Christians and people who have been believers for more than half a century. I have asked these questions also of some of the most famous Christians in the world. The answers are always the same, no matter who I ask.

1. What is the most important experience of your life?

    "Knowing Christ as my Savior."

2. What is the most important thing you can do for another person?

    "Help him or her to know Christ."

If you are a Christian, you undoubtedly would give the same answers to these questions. Yet if you are like the majority of Christians today, you have never introduced anyone to Christ. But you would like to do so, and you know in your heart that this is what God called you to do.

Bible Study

What Is a Witness?

1. Describe what a witness testifies to in a courtroom.

How is that like sharing your faith in Christ?

2. What are you admonished to do in Psalm 107:2 (use *The Living Bible*)?

Why is this hard for you to do?

3. How have you followed this admonishment today?

This week?

This month?

If you have not, what is keeping you from witnessing?

The Motivation for Witnessing

1. What did Jesus command you to do (Mark 16:15; Matthew 28:19,20)?

2. Read Acts 20:24–27,31,32.

How important would you say Paul's ministry of witnessing was to him?

Why?

3. Read 2 Corinthians 5:14,15.

What caused Paul to witness?

What attitude should we have about what Jesus has done for us?

How should that change our lives?

4. What does Jesus Christ say about the one who is ashamed of Him (Luke 9:26)?

How should this affect your witness?

5. If you are faithful to follow Jesus, what does He promise to do (Matthew 4:19)?

How has He helped you do this?

The Message

1. We are called Christ's ambassadors in 2 Corinthians 5:18–20. (An ambassador is one who is appointed to represent his country in a foreign land.) Reflect on the duties of an ambassador.

How do these relate to the Christian life and to witnessing about your faith in Christ?

2. Why did Jesus say He came into this world (Luke 19:10; Mark 10:45)?

3. As a representative of Christ, what would be your message to those who do not know Him personally? Write your answer in words you could use with a non-Christian.

4. How does Paul express the message in 1 Corinthians 15:3,4?

L I F E   A P P L I C A T I O N

1 Take several moments to reflect on what your relationship with Jesus Christ means to you. Complete this
statement:

Because Christ rose from the dead and lives in me, I...

Isn't this truly the greatest, most joyful news you could
ever share with another person?

2 Based on your obedience to Christ's command to share
your faith with others, what conclusion do you think
He would draw about your love for Him?

3 Why do you believe it is important that you, personally,
be a witness for Christ?

4 Can you think of at least two people with whom God led
you to share Christ during the past week?

1)

2)

How did you respond?

How would you like to respond?

Jesus Shows How to Witness

Many devout Christians fail miserably in their efforts to introduce others to Christ simply because they do not know how to go about it.

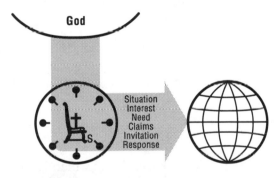

Knowing how to share your faith often makes the difference between effective and ineffective witnessing. Before you can introduce others to Christ, you must:

- ◆ Know that you are a Christian yourself
- ◆ Understand the empowering ministry of the Holy Spirit in your life personally
- ◆ Learn how to present the distilled essence of the gospel so simply, clearly, and convincingly that the one with whom you are sharing will be able to make an intelligent decision for Christ as Savior and Lord

Objective: To follow Christ's example in witnessing

Read: Galatians 3 and 4

Memorize: John 4:35

In this lesson we will observe Christ's example in witnessing. Jesus demonstrated how to witness in the most effective manner as He talked to the woman of Samaria. Study John 4 carefully to discover new approaches and techniques of witnessing.

Bible Study

Example of Jesus
Read John 4:1–42.

1. What everyday experience did Jesus use as an opportunity for witnessing?

2. What do you think is the advantage of beginning a conversation on the level of a person's immediate interest?

   Think of an occasion in which you used a person's special interest to share Christ with him. How did he respond?

3. List some of your natural opportunities to witness for Christ.

4. Why do you suppose Jesus sent all twelve of His disciples to buy provisions when two of them could have done it?

5. Who spoke first, Jesus or the woman of Samaria?

Why is this significant when considering how to witness?

6. What did Jesus do repeatedly when the woman tried to divert His attention from her sin and her need?

Responses of the Samaritan Woman

1. How did the woman first respond to Jesus' approach?

How does verse 15 indicate that her attitude changed?

What do you think brought it about?

2. What did Jesus say that demonstrated His divine powers?

3. How did Jesus describe God (verse 24)?

Why is this statement important?

4. Who was the woman looking for and why?

5. What did Jesus claim about Himself?

Effectiveness of Jesus' Witness

1. How effective was the approach Jesus used in witnessing to this woman of Samaria?

2. What was the result of His witness?

3. How did the people to whom she witnessed respond?

Why?

"Sound Barriers"

Sometimes witnessing can seem like breaking a sound barrier, like when an airplane accelerates to supersonic speed. Introducing the subject of Jesus can produce much stress and nervousness.

The *first sound barrier* occurs when we first mention the name of Jesus Christ and the value of knowing Him. Once we turn the conversation from dating, fashions, politics, work, sports, or any other topic to spiritual things, we have broken the first barrier. It is sometimes hard to do, and it does not always come easily.

The *second sound barrier* comes when we present the gospel. That nervous feeling returns once again. We must blast through this one also because many people, when they understand who Jesus Christ is and what He has done for them, *will* want Him in their lives.

The *last barrier,* asking the person to receive Christ right now, is the most difficult. But this is the most important step. Often we tell the person how to become a Christian and then just leave him high and dry. Until we ask the person to trust Christ as his or her Savior and Lord, our witness is not complete.

LIFE APPLICATION

1 Think of the last time you encountered the first barrier. How did you begin your conversation about Christ?

How could you have handled it better?

2 How did the person respond when you asked him to receive Christ?

If the person did not receive Christ, how could you have been more effective in your approach?

3 What is the one thing you have learned from Christ's example that you can apply most in your own witnessing?

4 What do you think hinders your witnessing most?

List some practical ways you can overcome it.

Qualifications for Witnessing

Personal preparation is the key to becoming a successful witness.

The first step is to *be sure that you yourself are a Christian.* Commit your entire person —your intellect, your emotions, your will— to Him and receive the gift of God's love and forgiveness through the Lord Jesus Christ.

The second step is to *be sure there is no unconfessed sin in your life.* If some sinful attitude or action is hindering your fellowship with God, He cannot live through you, and you will not be a joyful Christian or a fruitful witness for Christ.

The third step is to *be filled with the Holy Spirit.* To be fruitful in your witness for Christ, you must appropriate by faith the fullness of God's Spirit. Invite the Holy Spirit to control and empower you—to enable you to live a holy, godly life by faith and to make you a fruitful witness for Him.

The fourth step is to *be prepared to communicate your faith in Christ.* Keeping Christ

Objective: To take spiritual inventory in preparation for witnessing

Read: Galatians 5 and 6

Memorize: Matthew 4:19

on the throne of your life as the Lord of your heart is the best preparation for communicating your faith.

Carefully study the eighth chapter of Acts. List the qualifications for witnessing. Ask the Holy Spirit to make these qualities real in your own life.

Bible Study

Philip's Opportunity
Read Acts 8:26–40.

> **1.** According to verses 26 and 27, why do you think God called Philip for this particular assignment?

> **2.** To whom did Philip witness (verse 27)?

> **3.** Who told Philip to join the chariot (verse 29)?

> Does the Holy Spirit lead us in this same way today?

> Describe an example from your life.

4. How did Philip respond?

5. How did Philip approach the man (verse 30)?

6. Was the man ready?

Why?

What was his response?

7. What Old Testament passage was the Ethiopian reading (verses 28,32,33)?

To whom did this refer?

8. What was Philip's message?

Philip's Qualifications

1. Philip demonstrated at least eight qualities that contributed to his effectiveness for Christ. Place the appropriate verses after the following words:

   ◆ Knowledge of the Word of God

   ◆ Boldness

   ◆ Compassion

   ◆ Humility

   ◆ Obedience

   ◆ Receptivity, sensitivity to guidance

   ◆ Tact

   ◆ Enthusiasm

2. Reflect on each of these qualities. How are they at work in your life?

   Which ones do you have difficulty with?

   List ways you could strengthen these areas.

Possible Hindrances to Our Witnessing

After each hindrance, describe how it affects your witnessing.

1. *Spiritual lethargy*

   If you are not excited about something, chances are you won't tell many people about it. For many Christians, the excitement of the Christian walk has been dulled by everyday distractions, materialistic pursuits, and unconfessed sin. Like the believers in Ephesus, these men and women have left their first love.

How it affects my witnessing:

2. *Lack of preparation*

Personal dedication to Christ and understanding how to witness and what to say are imperative. Preparing your heart through prayer gives you the right attitude and opens yourself to the power of the Holy Spirit.

How it affects my witnessing:

3. *Fear of man*

We possibly will be persecuted by unbelievers, as well as believers, but the fear of man will prove to be a snare (Proverbs 29:25). Christ said of those who feared to confess His name, "They loved the praise of men more than the praise of God."

How it affects my witnessing:

4. *Fear of failure*

"They won't believe; they won't accept such simple truth." Certainly some will reject or neglect the gospel, but you should never believe the lie of Satan that people are not interested. Christ said, "Open your eyes and look at the fields! They are [present tense...'now'] ripe for harvest" (John 4:35).

Jesus said, "The harvest is plentiful but the workers are few. Ask the Lord...to send out workers into his harvest field" (Matthew 9:37,38).

How it affects my witnessing:

5. *Fear that the new Christian will not go on and grow in the Lord*

Review the parable of the sower (Matthew 13:1–23). Every seed of the Word of God will fall on one of these types of soil: path, rocky, thorny, or good. Some new Christians will become disciples. Keep up the faithful search for these disciples!

How it affects my witnessing:

6. *Lack of practical "know-how"*

As a result of thousands of surveys, we have found that the vast majority of Christians today not only believe they should share their faith, but they also really want to. However, they don't receive the practical hands-on training that will ease their fears and help them witness effectively. The result is a guilt trip: They know they should, but they hesitate because they don't know how.

How it affects my witnessing:

LIFE APPLICATION

1 Which hindrance is the greatest problem for you?

Why?

What steps will you take to overcome it?

2 Have you let distractions, lethargy, materialism, or unconfessed sin rob you of your excitement in Christ? In what ways?

3 In a time of quiet prayer, ask God to reveal any unconfessed sin in your life. After reading 1 John 1:9, confess any such sin, and ask for God's cleansing and forgiveness.

4 Look back through the list of qualities in Philip's life and identify the ones you would like to have God develop in your life.

5 Spend some time in prayer, asking God for those characteristics to be developed in your life and witness.

Witnessing and the Word of God

W hen the early Christians received the power of the Holy Spirit at Pentecost, the news spread quickly throughout Jerusalem, and a large crowd gathered, seeking the meaning of this phenomenon. Peter, under the control and in the power of the Holy Spirit, addressed the inquisitive crowd.

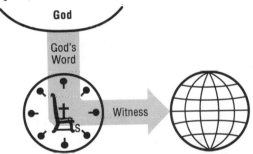

Who were these people? Some had been present at the crucifixion earlier and had cried, "Crucify Him" and, "Let his blood be on us and on our children" (Matthew 27:22, 25). Possibly some in the front row were those before whom Peter had used profanity when he denied Christ (Matthew 26:73,74).

Under these fearful circumstances, Peter's resources had to be God's Word, prayer, and the Holy Spirit. The purpose of this lesson is to demonstrate the use of the Word of God in witnessing, and its results.

Objective: To learn to use the power of God's Word in witnessing

Read: Ephesians 1 and 2

Memorize: 1 Peter 3:15

Bible Study

Peter's Witness

Read Acts 2.

1. Of all the disciples, why was Peter the least qualified to witness for Christ, and yet the most qualified, as suggested above and in Acts 2?

2. How much of Peter's sermon involves quotations from the Bible (such as from Joel, David, etc.)?

   How much Scripture memorization do you suppose Peter had done in his early life?

3. What part does the Holy Spirit play...
   In those who share Christ's message (John 14:26)?

   In those who hear Christ's message (John 16:8–11)?

4. What part does prayer play (Acts 2:42–47)?

5. What did Peter say to convince them of sin (Acts 2:23,36)?

6. List some great things Peter preached about God (verses 24,34,35,38,39).

The Crowd's Response

1. How many became Christians that day?

2. List the emotions experienced by the hearers before and after conversion.

3. Why did some listeners react in anger first?

The Power of the Word

1. Summarize Isaiah 55:11.

2. According to Hebrews 4:12, how does the Word of God affect the non-Christian as you witness?

3. In Ephesians 6:17, what is the Bible called?

Why?

As you will see in more detail in Lesson 6, it is the Holy Spirit who brings men to grips with the issues as we witness.

The Value of Scripture Memorization

Committing portions of Scripture to memory is the best way to know the Word of God, and as a result, to know Christ. Also, by having the promises and commands of the Word memorized, we can apply them to any life situation at a moment's notice, especially when we want to use them in an unexpected witnessing opportunity.

1. List some things God has promised us (2 Peter 1:2–4):

2. List some ways that memorizing Scripture will help you, according to the following verses:

1 Peter 2:2,3 and Hebrews 5:12–14

Joshua 1:8 and Psalm 1:1–3

Psalm 32:8

3. List some ways, mentioned in the following references, in which God's Word will nourish your growth:

Romans 10:17

Psalm 119:11

Psalm 119:165

4. Name one thing for which God's Word was absolutely essential, according to 1 Peter 1:23.

LIFE APPLICATION

1 List specific ways in which the preceding Bible verses will help you in your witnessing.

2 Which verse do you believe you need the most?

3 Memorize that passage.

4 How will you apply it?

❖ ❖ ❖

Witnessing and Prayer

Do you want your loved ones, your friends, and neighbors to come to Christ? Begin to claim them for God as you pray. Follow the example of our Lord, our High Priest, whose prayer is recorded in John 17:20: "My prayer is not for them alone. I pray also for those who will believe in me through their message."

Just as Jesus prayed that the Holy Spirit would work in the lives of His disciples, so we can pray that the Holy Spirit will convict non-believers and give them a strong desire to know God. Paul and other writers of the New Testament were frequently requesting prayer for others as well as for themselves.

Although God wants everyone to come to repentance, He chooses to wait for the prayers of a concerned believer to release the Holy Spirit in that person's heart. In our ef-

Objective: To make prayer a vital part of witnessing

Read: Ephesians 3 and 4

Memorize: Acts 4:31

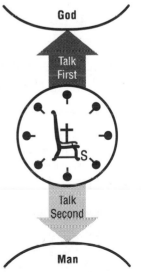

forts to lead people to Christ, we must first talk to God about men, then talk to men about God. If we follow this divine order, we will see results.

Since it is God's will that none should perish, and since God promises to answer any prayer offered in accordance with His will (1 John 5:14,15), we can know with assurance that God will answer our prayers for the salvation of souls for whom He has impressed us to pray (Philippians 2:13).

Prayer is really the place where people are won to Christ; sharing the Good News is just gathering in the fruit.

The aim of this lesson is to demonstrate that prayer played a major part in the witness of the early church.

Bible Study

What the Early Christians Prayed For

Read Acts 4.

1. What problem did these Christians face?

2. What do you think would have happened to Christianity if they had stopped witnessing?

3. How important is the soul-winning witness to the cause of Christ today? Give two specific examples.

1)

2)

4. How did these Christians solve their dilemma: Before magistrates?

In private?

In public?

5. What protected them (Acts 4:21)?

6. For what did they pray?

The Answer to Their Prayer

The answer to their prayer was immediate and definite. They prayed, and God answered as He had promised. None could stand against them, and they were victorious in Christ.

1. How can you profit from their courage, prayer, and effective witness?

2. Successful praying is simply asking God to work according to His will and leaving the results to Him. From this statement, what part does faith play in your prayers?

3. In what ways can other people depend on your courage, prayer, and witness?

4. Someone has said, "Prayer is not an argument with God to persuade Him to move things our way, but an exercise by which we are enabled by His Spirit to move ourselves His way."

How does this statement help us understand our role in witnessing?

In our willingness to share our faith?

The Christian's Opposition

1. How were the witnessing Christians of the early church persecuted? (The Book of Acts gives several examples.)

2. In your opinion, who is the author of resistance to Christian witness?

Why?

How does knowing this help you have more courage?

God's Timing

1. Success in witnessing is simply taking the initiative to share Christ in the power of the Holy Spirit and leaving the results to God.

   How do you react when a person does not receive the gospel right away?

   How should you react?

2. God's will does not operate according to our timetable. Think of a situation when God's answer to your prayer did not come at the time you expected. How did He answer that prayer?

   Relate the timing of this incident to waiting on God for His harvest.

LIFE APPLICATION

1 What specific opposition have you encountered recently, and how did you deal with it?

2 How could you have handled it better?

3 Which special friends or loved ones have been on your heart recently?

Have you ever felt that a particular situation was hopeless?

How can prayer change that attitude?

4 Look up verses that you can use when you feel a situation is hopeless. Put these verses on a card in your Bible so you can review them and pray over them the next time you get discouraged about witnessing. Use the index in your Bible to find appropriate verses.

5 What principles have you learned from this study to help you in your prayer and witness to these people?

Think of each person by name and apply the principles you have learned to each situation.

6 List at least one prospective witnessing situation and spend a few moments praying specifically for God's leading and empowering through your life.

7 Continue to pray without ceasing, but instead of begging and pleading with God, thank and praise Him by faith that He is going to answer your prayer in His perfect timing.

❖ ❖ ❖

Witnessing and the Holy Spirit

When you talk about Jesus, expect God to use you. The Lord Jesus promised His supernatural resources to all who join with Him in helping to fulfill the Great Commission.

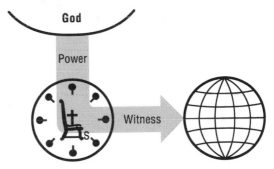

You are assured of that same resurrection power and presence today through the power of the Holy Spirit. Our Lord honors the faithful witness of all who place their trust in Him.

Self-consciousness and fear of what others will say, however, will hinder our witness. Stephen was a table waiter (Acts 6:2–5), not an apostle. He was brought before the most wicked opponents of Christianity. He could have retreated because he felt inadequate to face these people, but he yielded to the Holy Spirit's control of his life. As a result,

Objective: To understand and trust in the Holy Spirit's leading as you witness

Read: Ephesians 5 and 6

Memorize: John 15:26, 27

his faithfulness to Christ, even to accepting death by stoning, mightily moved the unbelievers and laid the basis for Saul's conversion.

Bible Study

Work of the Holy Spirit in a Believer's Life

Read Acts 6 and 7, and underline every mention of the Holy Spirit.

1. What part did the Holy Spirit play in Stephen's life?

2. What spiritual indictment did Stephen pronounce upon his hearers that cut them to the heart?

3. As a Spirit-filled man, Stephen had two purposes that were his greatest concerns, as seen in his desire to witness and in his dying prayer. What were they?

1)

2)

4. How do these concerns show the fullness of the Holy Spirit in Stephen? (Compare Galatians 5:22,23; 2 Corinthians 5:14,15.)

Work of the Holy Spirit in Witnessing

1. What is the ministry of the Holy Spirit (John 15:26; 16:13,14)?

2. How is it accomplished in a person who witnesses of Christ (Acts 1:8; 6:10)?

How is it being accomplished in your life?

3. What will the Holy Spirit do for the witnessing person (Acts 4:31)?

4. What will the Holy Spirit do for the person receiving the Good News (1 Corinthians 2:10–12)?

5. How does that passage compare with 2 Corinthians 4:3,4?

6. It is the Holy Spirit who brings us face to face with the facts regarding our condition and our need. This action is called "convicting, reproving, exposing, bringing to light."

If we were to witness on our own, we would accomplish nothing. But when the Holy Spirit uses our witness, He brings a person face to face with important facts, presenting them so forcefully that these facts must be considered.

What are these facts (John 16:7–11)?

7. What promise does God give us regarding His Spirit (2 Corinthians 1:21,22)?

LIFE APPLICATION

1 Record the names of at least three persons to whom you believe God would have you speak about Christ within the next week.

1)

2)

3)

2 Ask the Holy Spirit to prepare these individuals, freeing their minds so they can make a logical, intelligent choice to receive Christ as Savior.

3 Study "How to Share Christ With Others" on pages 65–67. Practice reading through the *Four Spiritual Laws* booklet with a friend.

4 Ask the Holy Spirit to lead you to these individuals at the proper time, and to speak through you in giving them the message of Christ.

As you witness, remember that it is the Holy Spirit who penetrates the mind of the other person, revealing spiritual truth.

5 Are you sure you are prepared? If not, review the earlier lessons in this Step.

Recap

The following questions will help you review this Step. If necessary, reread the appropriate lesson(s).

1. What is the most important reason you have learned to witness for Christ?

2. How have you overcome the problem that most hinders your witnessing?

Reread: Galatians and Ephesians

Review: Verses memorized

3. What is the next most troubling hindrance for you, and how do you plan to overcome it?

4. Summarize why you think a knowledge of the Word of God is important in witnessing.

5. How will prayer specifically help you?

6. Why do you think the Holy Spirit does not speak of Himself?

LIFE APPLICATION

1 Write a three-minute testimony of your personal experience with Christ. Briefly share three things:

1) What your life was like before your decision

2) Why and how you received Christ

3) How Christ has changed your life

List benefits of knowing Christ. Explain in greater detail what it is like to be a Christian. (Attach your testimony to this lesson.)

2 Begin a prayer diary listing those whom God has laid on your heart to share your faith in Christ.

Record:

◆ Their prayer needs

◆ Their responses to your witness

◆ Their spiritual growth

3 List the opportunities God has given you to witness for Him in the past month. Then praise and thank God for them.

A Challenge

Some years ago, a disarmament conference was held in England. In the midst of a speech by King George, someone tripped over the wires of the Columbia Broadcasting Company, tearing them loose and interrupting the broadcast. The chief operator quickly grasped the loose wires in his bare hands and held them in contact.

For twenty minutes, the current passed through him while repairs were being made. His hands were slightly burned, but through them the words of the king passed on to millions of listeners.

Without the operator's courage and endurance, the king's message would have failed to reach its destination.

Jesus Christ, the King of kings, has chosen to send His message of salvation to a lost and dying world through human means. Whatever the cost, the message must reach those who have never heard it. Every faithful and willing Christian is a human instrument through whom the King's voice is reaching the lost.

Obedience to our Lord's call brings great promise:

Those who are wise—the people of God—shall shine as brightly as the sun's brilliance, and those who turn

Whatever the cost, the message must reach those who have never heard it.

many to righteousness will glitter like stars forever (Daniel 12:3, TLB).

Successful witnessing is simply taking the initiative to share Christ in the power of the Holy Spirit, and leaving the results to God.

No other experience in this world can compare with that of witnessing for Christ in the power of the Holy Spirit and leaving the results to God. Will you join me in this great adventure?

How to Share Christ With Others

A well-known Christian leader, highly gifted as a theologian, shared with me his frustration over his lack of effectiveness and fruitfulness in witnessing for Christ.

I asked him, "What do you say when you seek to introduce a person to Christ?"

He explained his presentation, which was long and complicated. The large number of Bible verses he used would confuse most people and prevent them from making an intelligent decision.

I challenged him to use the *Four Spiritual Laws* presentation daily for the next thirty days and report his progress to me at the end of that time.

When I saw him two weeks later, he was overflowing with joy and excitement. "By simply reading the booklet to others," he said, "I have seen more people come to Christ during the last two weeks than I had previously seen in many months. It's hard to believe!"

The *Four Spiritual Laws*[1] booklet, reproduced on pages 70 through 76, presents a clear and simple explanation of the gospel of our Lord Jesus Christ.

❖

The *Four Spiritual Laws* presents a clear and simple explanation of the gospel.

---

[1] The *Four Spiritual Laws* booklet can be obtained by writing NewLife Publications, 100 Sunport Lane, Orlando, FL 32809.

This booklet, available in all major languages of the world, has been developed as a result of more than forty years of experience in counseling with thousands of college students on campuses in almost every country on every continent in the world, as well as with a comparable number of laymen, pastors, and high school students. It represents one way to share your faith effectively.

Benefits of *Four Laws*

Using a tool such as the *Four Spiritual Laws* offers many benefits. Let me list some of them:

- ◆ It enables you to open your conversation easily and naturally.
- ◆ It begins with a positive statement: "God loves you and has a wonderful plan for your life."
- ◆ It presents the gospel and the claims of Christ clearly and simply.
- ◆ It gives you confidence because you know what you are going to say and how you are going to say it.
- ◆ It enables you to be prepared at all times and to stick to the subject without getting off on tangents.
- ◆ It makes it possible for you to be brief and to the point.
- ◆ It enables you to lead others to a personal decision through a suggested prayer.
- ◆ It offers suggestions for growth, including the importance of involvement in the church.
- ◆ Of special importance, it is a "transferable tool" to give those whom you introduce to Christ so they can be encouraged and trained to lead others to Christ also. Paul exhorted Timothy, his young son in the faith:

    The things you have heard me say in the presence of many witnesses entrust to reliable men who will also be qualified to teach others (2 Timothy 2:2).

The *Four Spiritual Laws* enables those who receive Christ to go immediately to friends and loved ones and tell them of their new-found faith in Christ. It also enables them to show their friends and loved ones how they, too, can make a commitment to Christ.

Various Approaches

You can introduce the *Four Spiritual Laws* to a non-believer. After a cordial, friendly greeting, you can use one of the following approaches:

- ◆ "I'm reading a little booklet that really makes sense to a lot of people. I'd like to share it with you. Have you heard of the *Four Spiritual Laws?*"

- ◆ "Do you ever think about spiritual things?" (Pause for an answer.) "Have you ever heard of the *Four Spiritual Laws?*"

- ◆ "A friend of mine recently gave me this little booklet that really makes sense to me. I would like to share it with you. Have you ever heard of the *Four Spiritual Laws?*"

- ◆ "The content of this booklet has been used to change the lives of millions of people. It contains truths that I believe will be of great interest to you. Would you read it and give me your impression?"

- ◆ "It is believed that this little booklet is the most widely printed piece of literature in the world apart from the Bible.[2] Would you be interested in reading it?"

Here is a direct approach that you can use when you have only a few moments with an individual:

> "If you died today, do you know for sure that you will go to heaven?"

If the answer is yes, ask:

> "On what do you base that knowledge? This little booklet, the *Four Spiritual Laws*, will help you know for sure that you will go to heaven when you die."

If the answer is no, say:

> "You *can* be sure you are going to heaven. This little booklet, the *Four Spiritual Laws*, tells how to know."

God will show you other ways to introduce this material. The important thing is to keep your introduction brief and to the point.

---

[2] It is estimated that over one-and-a-half billion *Four Spiritual Laws* booklets have been printed and distributed in all major languages of the world.

How to Present the Four Spiritual Laws

1. Be sensitive to an individual's interest and the leading of the Holy Spirit. The simplest way to explain the *Four Spiritual Laws* is to read the booklet aloud to a non-believer. But be careful not to allow the presentation to become mechanical. Remember, you are not just sharing principles, you are introducing the person to Christ. The *Four Spiritual Laws* is simply a tool to help you effectively communicate the gospel. Pray for God's love to be expressed through you.

2. If there is any objection to the term "laws," use the term "Four Spiritual Principles" instead.[3]

3. When questions arise that would change the subject, explain that most questions are answered as you go through the *Four Spiritual Laws.* Or say, "That's a good question. Let's talk about it after we have completed reading the booklet."

4. Be sensitive to the individual. If he doesn't seem to respond, stop and ask, "Is this making sense?"

❖

Millions have received Christ through reading the *Four Spiritual Laws.*

---

[3] You may want to use an adaption of the *Four Spiritual Laws* entitled *Would You Like to Know God Personally?* It is available through your local Christian bookstore, mail-order catalog distributor, or NewLife Publications.

5. Hold the booklet so the individual can see it clearly. Use a pen to point to key areas. This will help hold his attention.

6. In a group, give each person a *Four Spiritual Laws* booklet. Pray with those who are interested in receiving Christ. If only one is interested, be sensitive and in most cases talk with that person privately. Make sure each one understands that Christ comes into his life by faith. If he prays the prayer without believing Christ will answer, nothing will result.

   Also be sensitive about whether he wants to pray his own prayer or use the prayer from the booklet. Some will request silent prayer.

7. If someone has already heard of the *Four Spiritual Laws*, ask him what he thought of them, and if he has any questions. If he is interested and the gospel is not clear to him, go over the booklet again.

8. When a person does not receive Christ when you first share the *Four Spiritual Laws* with him, make another appointment if he is interested. Give him the booklet *A Great Adventure* to take with him. (The booklet is available at your Christian bookstore or can be ordered through NewLife Publications.)

9. Pray for the person. Occasionally ask him if he has thought further about your discussion or if he has any questions.

10. Leave the *Four Spiritual Laws* or *A Great Adventure* with the person you have witnessed to whether or not he received Christ. Millions have received Christ through reading these booklets.

Have You Heard
of the
Four Spiritual Laws?

Just as there are physical laws that govern the physical universe, so are there spiritual laws that govern your relationship with God.

LAW ONE

GOD **LOVES** YOU AND HAS A WONDERFUL **PLAN** FOR YOUR LIFE.

God's Love

God so loved the world that He gave His only begotten Son, that whoever believes in Him should not perish, but have eternal life (John 3:16).

God's Plan

[Christ speaking] "I came that they might have life, and might have it abundantly" [that it might be full and meaningful] (John 10:10).

Why is it that most people are not experiencing the abundant life?

Because...

LAW TWO

MAN IS **SINFUL** AND **SEPARATED** FROM GOD. THUS HE CANNOT KNOW AND EXPERIENCE GOD'S LOVE AND PLAN FOR HIS LIFE.

Man Is Sinful

All have sinned and fall short of the glory of God (Romans 3:23).

Man was created to have fellowship with God; but, because of his own stubborn self-will, he chose to go his own independent way and fellowship with God was broken. This self-will, characterized by an attitude of active rebellion or passive indifference, is an evidence of what the Bible calls sin.

Man Is Separated

The wages of sin is death [spiritual separation from God] (Romans 6:23).

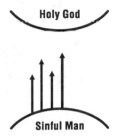

This diagram illustrates that God is holy and man is sinful. A great chasm separates the two. The arrows illustrate that man is continually trying to reach God and the abundant life through his own efforts: good life, ethics, philosophy, and more.

The Third Law gives us the only answer to this dilemma...

LAW THREE

JESUS CHRIST IS GOD'S **ONLY** PROVISION FOR MAN'S SIN. THROUGH HIM YOU CAN KNOW AND EXPERIENCE GOD'S LOVE AND PLAN FOR YOUR LIFE.

He Died In Our Place

God demonstrates His own love toward us, in that while we were yet sinners, Christ died for us (Romans 5:8).

He Rose from the Dead

Christ died for our sins... He was buried... He was raised on the third day, according to the Scriptures... He appeared to Peter, then to the twelve. After that He appeared to more than five hundred... (1 Corinthians 15:3–6).

He Is the Only Way to God

> Jesus said to him, "I am the way, and the truth, and the life; no one comes to the Father but through Me" (John 14:6).

This diagram illustrates that God has bridged the chasm that separates us from Him by sending His Son, Jesus Christ, to die on the cross in our place to pay the penalty for our sins.

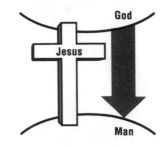

It is not enough to know these three laws...

LAW FOUR

WE MUST INDIVIDUALLY **RECEIVE** JESUS CHRIST AS SAVIOR AND LORD; THEN WE CAN KNOW AND EXPERIENCE GOD'S LOVE AND PLAN FOR OUR LIVES.

We Must Receive Christ

> As many as received Him, to them He gave the right to become children of God, even to those who believe in His name (John 1:12).

We Receive Christ Through Faith

> By grace you have been saved through faith; and that not of yourselves, it is the gift of God; not as a result of works that no one should boast (Ephesians 2:8,9).

When We Receive Christ, We Experience a New Birth
(Read John 3:1–8.)

We Receive Christ Through Personal Invitation

> [Christ speaking] "Behold, I stand at the door and knock; if any one hears My voice and opens the door, I will come in to him" (Revelation 3:20).

Receiving Christ involves turning to God from self (repentance) and trusting Christ to come into our lives to forgive our sins and to make us what He wants us to be. Just to agree intellectually that Jesus Christ is the Son of God and that He died on the cross for our sins is not enough. Nor is it enough to have an emotional experience. We receive Jesus Christ by faith, as an act of the will.

These two circles represent two kinds of lives:

Self-Directed Life
S – Self is on the throne
† – Christ is outside the life
● – Interests are directed by self, often resulting in discord and frustration

Christ-Directed Life
† – Christ is in the life and on the throne
S – Self is yielding to Christ
● – Interests are directed by Christ, resulting in harmony with God's plan

Which circle best represents your life?

Which circle would you like to have represent your life?

The following explains how you can receive Christ:

You Can Receive Christ Right Now by Faith Through Prayer
(Prayer is talking with God)

God knows your heart and is not so concerned with your words as He is with the attitude of your heart. The following is a suggested prayer:

> *Lord Jesus, I need You. Thank You for dying on the cross for my sins. I open the door of my life and receive You as my Savior and Lord. Thank You for forgiving my sins and giving me eternal life. Take control of the throne of my life. Make me the kind of person You want me to be.*

Does this prayer express the desire of your heart?

If it does, pray this prayer right now, and Christ will come into your life, as He promised.

How to Know That Christ Is in Your Life

Did you receive Christ into your life? According to His promise in Revelation 3:20, where is Christ right now in relation to you?

Christ said that He would come into your life. Would He mislead you? On what authority do you know that God has answered your prayer? (The trustworthiness of God Himself and His Word.)

The Bible Promises Eternal Life to All Who Receive Christ

> The witness is this, that God has given us eternal life, and this life is in His Son. He who has the Son has the life; he who does not have the Son of God does not have the life. These things I have written to you who believe in the name of the Son of God, in order that you may know that you have eternal life (1 John 5:11–13).

Thank God often that Christ is in your life and that He will never leave you (Hebrews 13:5). You can know on the basis of His promise that the living Christ indwells you and that you have eternal life from the very moment you invite Him in. He will not deceive you.

An important reminder...

Do Not Depend on Feelings

The promise of God's Word, the Bible—not our feelings—is our authority. The Christian lives by faith (trust) in the trustworthiness of God Himself and His Word. This train diagram illustrates the relationship between **fact** (God and His Word), **faith** (our trust in God and His Word), and **feeling** (the result of our faith and obedience). (Read John 14:21.)

The train will run with or without the caboose. However, it would be useless to attempt to pull the train by the caboose. In the same way, as Christians we do not depend on feelings or emotions, but we place our faith (trust) in the trustworthiness of God and the promises of His Word.

Now That You Have Received Christ

The moment you received Christ by faith, as an act of the will, many things happened, including the following:

- ◆ Christ came into your life (Revelation 3:20; Colossians 1:27).
- ◆ Your sins were forgiven (Colossians 1:14).
- ◆ You became a child of God (John 1:12).
- ◆ You received eternal life (John 5:24).
- ◆ You began the great adventure for which God created you (John 10:10; 2 Corinthians 5:17; 1 Thessalonians 5:18).

Can you think of anything more wonderful that could happen to you than receiving Christ? Would you like to thank God in prayer right now for what He has done for you? By thanking God, you demonstrate your faith.

To enjoy your new life to the fullest...

Suggestions for Christian Growth

Spiritual growth results from trusting Jesus Christ. "The righteous man shall live by faith" (Galatians 3:11). A life of faith will enable you to trust God increasingly with every detail of your life, and to practice the following:

- **G** Go to God in prayer daily (John 15:7).
- **R** Read God's Word daily (Acts 17:11); begin with the Gospel of John.
- **O** Obey God moment by moment (John 14:21).
- **W** Witness for Christ by your life and words (Matthew 4:19; John 15:8).
- **T** Trust God for every detail of your life (1 Peter 5:7).
- **H** Holy Spirit—allow Him to control and empower your daily life and witness (Galatians 5:16,17; Acts 1:8).

Fellowship in a Good Church

God's Word admonishes us not to forsake "the assembling of ourselves together" (Hebrews 10:25). Several logs burn brightly together, but put one aside on the cold hearth and the fire goes out. So it is with your relationship with other Christians.

If you do not belong to a church, do not wait to be invited. Take the initiative; call the pastor of a nearby church where Christ is honored and His Word is preached. Start this week, and make plans to attend regularly.

Resources to Help You Witness

A Man Without Equal. A fresh look at the unique birth, teachings, death, and resurrection of Jesus and how He continues to change the way we live and think. Good as an evangelistic tool.

Witnessing Without Fear. A step-by-step guide to sharing your faith with confidence. Ideal for both individual and group study; a Gold Medallion winner.

Four Spiritual Laws. One of the most effective evangelistic tools ever developed. An easy-to-use way of sharing your faith with others.

Would You Like to Know God Personally? An adaptation of the *Four Spiritual Laws* presented as four principles for establishing a personal relationship with God through faith in Jesus Christ.

Spirit-Filled Life booklet. Discover the reality of the Spirit-filled life and how to live in moment-by-moment dependence on Him.

Transferable Concepts. Exciting tools to help you experience and share the abundant Christian life:

How You Can Be a Fruitful Witness

How You Can Introduce Others to Christ

How You Can Help Fulfill the Great Commission

Ten Basic Steps. A comprehensive curriculum for the Christian who wants to master the basics of Christian growth. Used by hundreds of thousands worldwide. (See page 79 for details.)

The Ten Basic Steps Leader's Guide. Contains Bible study outlines for teaching the complete series.

The Handbook for Christian Maturity. Combines the entire series of the *Ten Basic Steps* in one volume. A handy resource for private Bible study, an excellent book to help nurture spiritual growth and maturity.

Reaching Your World Through Witnessing Without Fear. This powerful six-session video series can equip your church or small group to successfully share the gospel in a natural way through everyday relationships.

Practical, proven witnessing techniques are illustrated through exciting drama and in-depth training by Bill Bright.

Handy Facilitator's Guide enables lay-people to effectively lead training sessions.

Available through your local Christian bookstore, mail-order catalog distributor, or NewLife Publications.

Ten Basic Steps Toward Christian Maturity

Eleven easy-to-use individual guides to help you understand the basics of the Christian faith

INTRODUCTION: The Uniqueness of Jesus

Explains who Jesus Christ is. Reveals the secret of His power to turn you into a victorious, fruitful Christian.

STEP 1: The Christian Adventure

Shows you how to enjoy a full, abundant, purposeful, and fruitful life in Christ.

STEP 2: The Christian and the Abundant Life

Explores the Christian way of life— what it is and how it works practically.

STEP 3: The Christian and the Holy Spirit

Teaches who the Holy Spirit is, how to be filled with the Spirit, and how to make the Spirit-filled life a moment-by-moment reality in your life.

STEP 4: The Christian and Prayer

Reveals the true purpose of prayer and shows how the Father, Son, and Holy Spirit work together to answer your prayers.

STEP 5: The Christian and the Bible

Talks about the Bible—how we got it, its authority, and its power to help the believer. Offers methods for studying the Bible more effectively.

STEP 6: The Christian and Obedience

Learn why it is so important to obey God and how to live daily in His grace. Discover the secret to personal purity and power as a Christian and why you need not fear what others think of you.

STEP 7: The Christian and Witnessing

Shows you how to witness effectively. Includes a reproduction of the *Four Spiritual Laws* and explains how to share them.

STEP 8: The Christian and Giving

Discover God's plan for your financial life, how to stop worrying about money, and how to trust God for your finances.

STEP 9: Exploring the Old Testament

Features a brief survey of the Old Testament. Shows what God did to prepare the way for Jesus Christ and the redemption of all who receive Him as Savior and Lord.

STEP 10: Exploring the New Testament

Surveys each of the New Testament books. Shows the essence of the gospel and highlights the exciting beginning of the Christian church

Leader's Guide

The ultimate resource for even the most inexperienced, timid, and fearful person asked to lead a group study in the basics of the Christian life. Contains questions and answers from the *Ten Basic Steps* Study Guides.

A Handbook for Christian Maturity

Combines the eleven-booklet series into one practical, easy-to-follow volume. Excellent for personal or group study.

Available through your local Christian bookstore, mail-order catalog distributor, or NewLife Publications.

About the Author

BILL BRIGHT is founder and president of Campus Crusade for Christ International. Serving in 152 major countries representing 98 percent of the world's population, he and his dedicated associates of nearly 50,000 full-time staff, associate staff, and trained volunteers have introduced tens of millions of people to Jesus Christ, discipling millions to live Spirit-filled, fruitful lives of purpose and power for the glory of God.

Dr. Bright did graduate study at Princeton and Fuller Theological seminaries from 1946 to 1951. The recipient of many national and international awards, including five honorary doctorates, he is the author of numerous books and publications committed to helping fulfill the Great Commission. His special focus is New Life 2000, an international effort to help reach more than six billion people with the gospel of our Lord Jesus Christ and help fulfill the Great Commission by the year 2000.